S0-CSX-319

?? ASK AN ?? ?
ANIMAL

olivia Brookes

PowerKiDS
press.

New York

Published in 2009 by The Rosen Publishing Group, Inc.
29 East 21st Street, New York, NY 10010

Copyright © 2009 Orpheus Books Ltd

All rights reserved. No part of this book may be
reproduced in any form without permission in writing
from the publisher, except by a reviewer.

Created and produced by: Julia Bruce,
Rachel Coombs, Nicholas Harris, Sarah Hartley, and
Erica Simms, Orpheus Books Ltd

Text: Olivia Brookes

U.S. editor: Kara Murray

Illustrated by: Ian Jackson (*The Art Agency*)
Other illustrations by: Mike Rowe, Peter David Scott
and David Wright

Consultant: Chris Jarvis
The Oxford University Museum
of Natural History, England

Library of Congress Cataloging-in-Publication Data

Brookes, Olivia.
An animal / Olivia Brookes.
p. cm. — (Ask)
Includes index.
ISBN 978-1-4358-2512-3 (library binding)
1. Animals—Miscellanea—Juvenile literature. I. Title.
QL49.B7463 2009
590—dc22
2008005549

Manufactured in China

contents

Introduction

We animals come in all shapes and sizes. We live on the land, in the water, or in the air. Some of us have fur, some have feathers, and some have scales. We all have stories about how we live our lives. From the hot sands of the Sahara Desert to the icy wastes of the Arctic, we have different ways of finding food, staying safe, finding a mate, and raising our young. You'll run with a cheetah and help a crocodile's egg hatch. You'll meet one of the fastest birds in the world (you might be surprised to learn who it is), find out from a camel what's really in its hump, and go on a hunt with a pride of lionesses. But first, an African elephant is waiting to tell you all the things it can do with its amazing trunk.

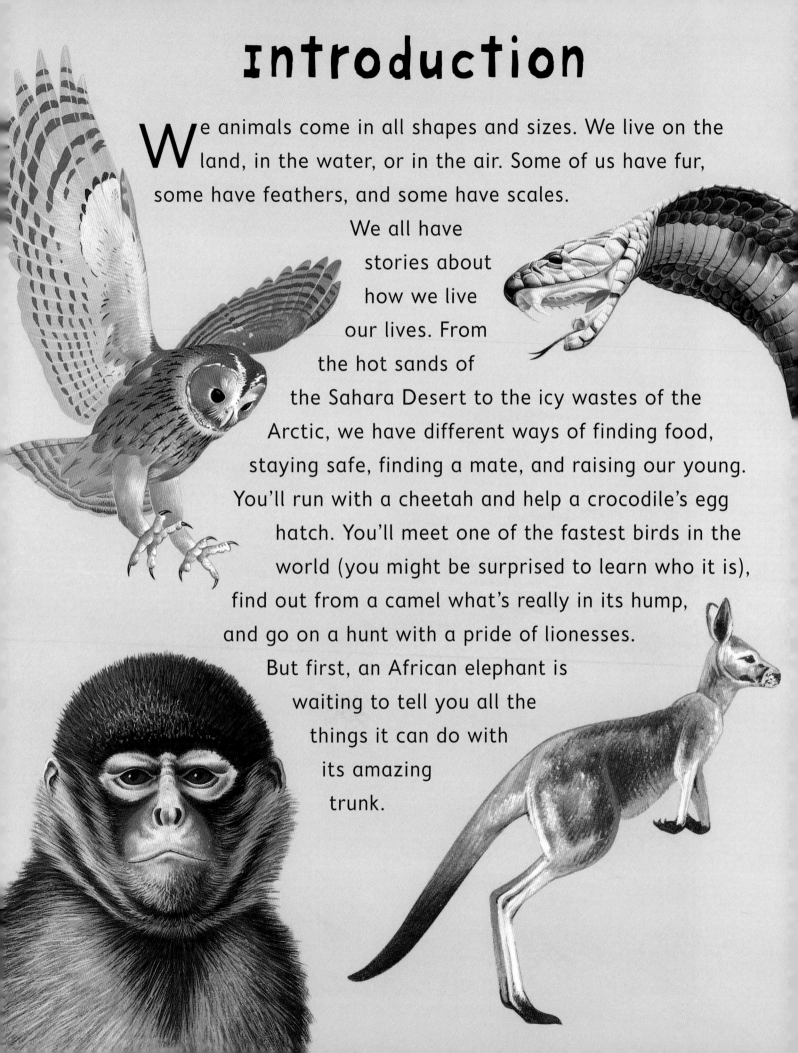

Why Do Elephants Have Trunks?

We African elephants use our trunks for many things. We can reach up to the treetops where the leaves are the tastiest. We can trumpet with it. We can even say hello to other elephants by touching them with it!

I can't bend down to drink water, so I suck it up through my trunk and spray it into my mouth.

I have two fingers at the tip of my trunk. Watch me pick up this leaf.

We are great swimmers, happy in the water from an early age.

When I swim, I poke my trunk out of the water like a snorkel. This allows me to breathe underwater.

My trunk is very strong. To lift this tree trunk out of my way, I wrap my trunk around it and lift.

Showers are fun! I suck up water and spray it over my back to cool off and to get clean.

Our trunks have no bones in them, which makes them very bendy. My trunk is tired after all this work today.

5

What's It Like Inside a Kangaroo's Pouch?

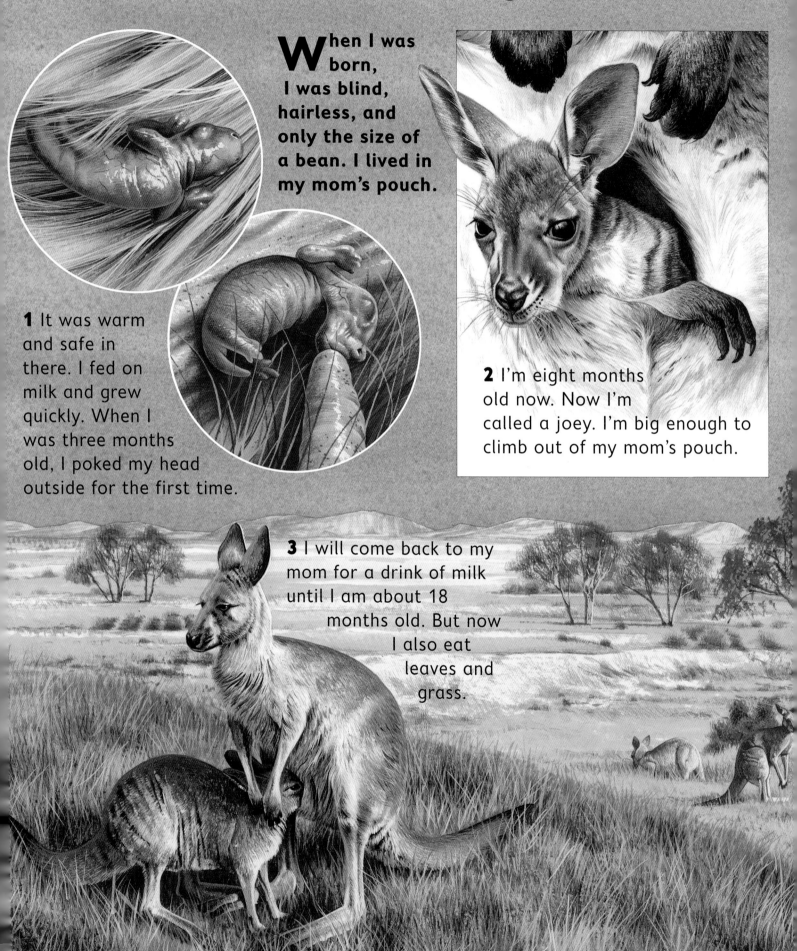

When I was born, I was blind, hairless, and only the size of a bean. I lived in my mom's pouch.

1 It was warm and safe in there. I fed on milk and grew quickly. When I was three months old, I poked my head outside for the first time.

2 I'm eight months old now. Now I'm called a joey. I'm big enough to climb out of my mom's pouch.

3 I will come back to my mom for a drink of milk until I am about 18 months old. But now I also eat leaves and grass.

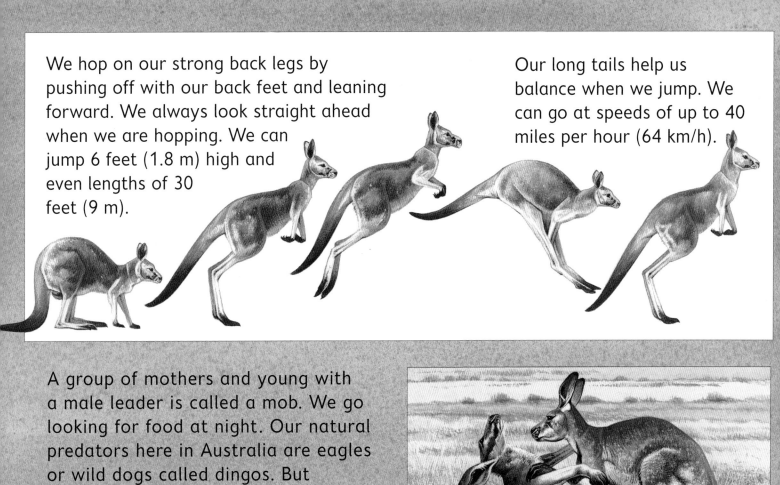

We hop on our strong back legs by pushing off with our back feet and leaning forward. We always look straight ahead when we are hopping. We can jump 6 feet (1.8 m) high and even lengths of 30 feet (9 m).

Our long tails help us balance when we jump. We can go at speeds of up to 40 miles per hour (64 km/h).

A group of mothers and young with a male leader is called a mob. We go looking for food at night. Our natural predators here in Australia are eagles or wild dogs called dingos. But humans are the most dangerous. We get hit by cars or shot by hunters.

Males will fight over females. They punch with their fists and kick with their legs.

We are called red kangaroos, but females are often gray.

Why Do Giraffes Have Long Necks?

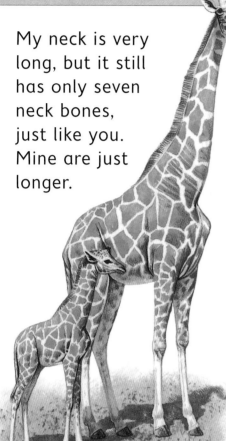

My neck is very long, but it still has only seven neck bones, just like you. Mine are just longer.

My baby is a few weeks old. He will nurse until he is one year old. Even when he's grown up, his neck will keep growing. A long neck is useful for fighting. When males hit each other with their heads, the one with the longer neck usually wins.

Here on the African savanna, animals, like me, are known as browsers because we eat leaves from trees and bushes. I'm a giraffe. I'm lucky to be so tall because I can reach the best new leaves from the treetops. Lots of us savanna animals eat plants, but we all eat different things—grass, leaves, fruit, and so on. That's how we can live together without fighting or going hungry.

This Cape eland is the largest African antelope. Using its horns, it pulls down or breaks off branches in order to eat the leaves.

Zebras eat the tough tops of the grass. Wildebeests, also called gnus, tear out the leafy middles. This makes room for little gazelles to reach the juiciest plants growing close to the ground.

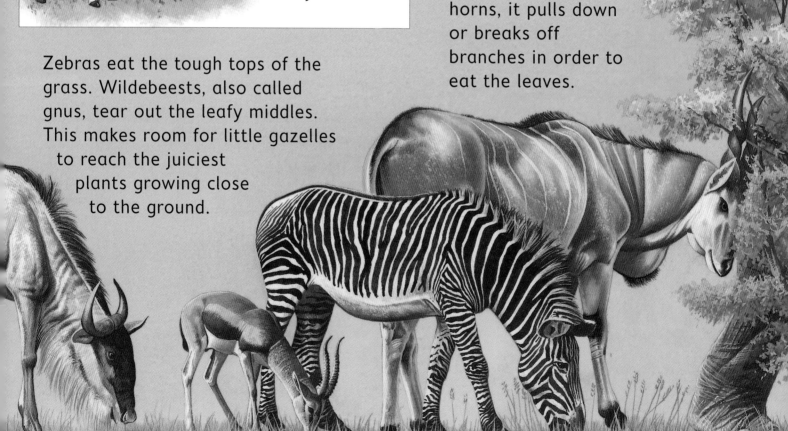

My neck is long, but so are my legs. I have to do this to drink water.

With my long, black tongue, I strip leaves from the treetops. So does the elephant, by using its trunk. The gerenuk stands on its hind legs to feed while the tiny dik dik eats leaves from the lowest branches.

The black rhinoceros uses its top lip to grab leaves, or even tree bark.

9

What Do Bears Like to Eat?

It's summer here in Alaska, and the salmon are swimming up the river to breed. There are so many of them, they are easy for us grizzly bears to catch. We will eat pretty much anything we can get our paws on: insects, frogs, small mammals, berries, roots, and even your leftover picnics if you leave them behind! We're not as cuddly as we look, either. In fact, we are very dangerous to humans. We can even hunt and kill large animals, like moose or caribou.

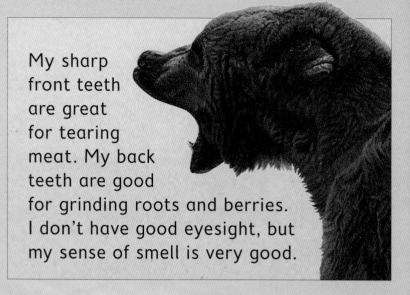

My sharp front teeth are great for tearing meat. My back teeth are good for grinding roots and berries. I don't have good eyesight, but my sense of smell is very good.

When these salmon leap out of the water going up the waterfall, I simply catch them in my mouth. Eating oily salmon helps me build up fat for my long winter hibernation.

A favorite treat for black bears is honey. I just found a beehive inside this tree. My thick fur protects me from those angry bees' stingers.

I am a polar bear from the frozen Arctic. I eat seals and fish. I'm waiting for a seal to come up through this hole in the ice to breathe. One swipe of my paw and this one's mine!

I am one of the rarest mammals in the world—a giant panda from China. I eat bamboo, but there is not much goodness in it, so I have to eat a lot of it. I spend most of my time sleeping or eating.

I have five normal toes, plus an extra thumb that helps me grab the narrow bamboo stems when I eat.

Do All Wild Cats Hunt Alone?

I am a cheetah, the fastest land animal alive. I have strong muscles, a slim body, and long legs. My bones are light, and I have a long stride, or step. My tail helps me to balance and turn quickly at high speeds. All this means I can hit a top speed of over 60 miles per hour (97 km/h). That's as fast as a car on the highway!

1 I can only keep up these high speeds for very short bursts, so I usually stalk my prey first. I need to get as close as possible before I dash in for the kill.

Our color and stripes help camouflage us tigers as we stalk our prey.

Crouching in the grass so my prey can't see or smell me, I slowly creep up on it. When I'm close enough, I attack!

2 I hunt in daytime and use my sharp eyes to spot my prey. The dark stripes under my eyes help me see clearly in bright sunshine. I kill my prey by biting its throat so it can't breathe.

A male lion rules our pride, but we lionesses do most of the hunting. Together in a pack, we can easily attack large animals, like this wildebeest. When it's surrounded, we move in for the kill. We share it with the pride.

I am a fishing cat. I live in the swamp forests of Malaysia. I eat frogs, shellfish, and fish. I sometimes dive headfirst into the water to catch them. Or I sit on the bank and gently tap the water's surface. When a curious fish comes by, I snatch it.

3 I won't need to hunt again for a day or two after such a big meal. I have to eat quickly before scavengers, such as hyenas or vultures, move in to eat what I've caught.

What Does a Monkey Use Its Tail For?

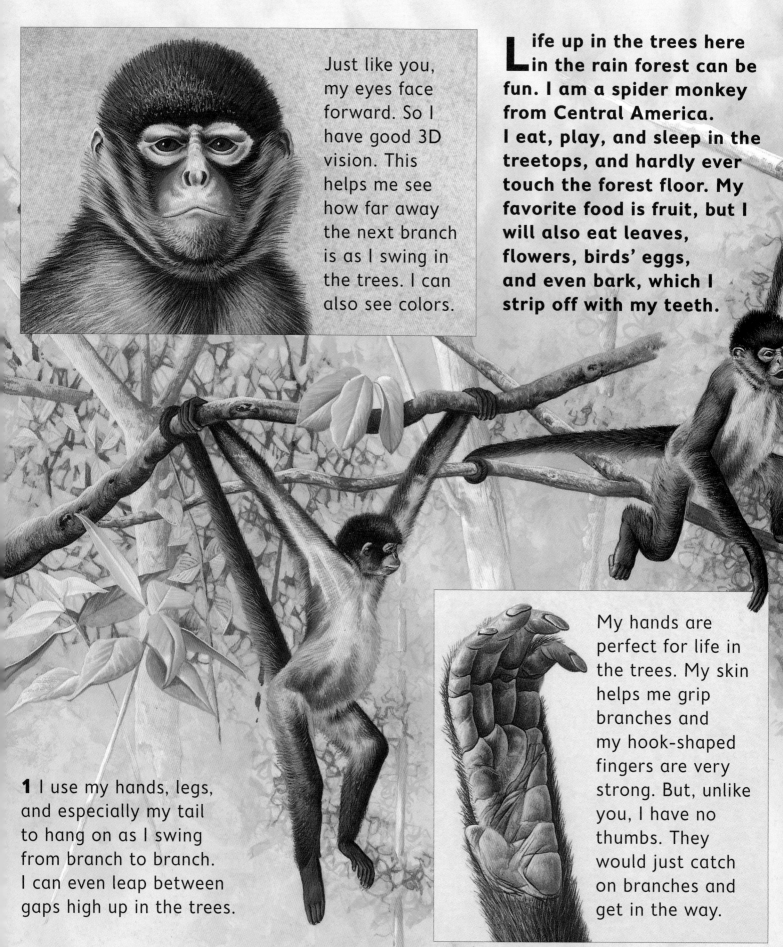

Just like you, my eyes face forward. So I have good 3D vision. This helps me see how far away the next branch is as I swing in the trees. I can also see colors.

Life up in the trees here in the rain forest can be fun. I am a spider monkey from Central America. I eat, play, and sleep in the treetops, and hardly ever touch the forest floor. My favorite food is fruit, but I will also eat leaves, flowers, birds' eggs, and even bark, which I strip off with my teeth.

1 I use my hands, legs, and especially my tail to hang on as I swing from branch to branch. I can even leap between gaps high up in the trees.

My hands are perfect for life in the trees. My skin helps me grip branches and my hook-shaped fingers are very strong. But, unlike you, I have no thumbs. They would just catch on branches and get in the way.

2 My tail also helps me balance when I leap between branches and walk high above ground. I use it like an extra, longer arm. It can reach farther than my arms or legs. It helps me move more quickly than if I just used my other limbs.

3 I push myself off a branch with my back legs and grab the next one with my tail. I don't even have to think about what to do next.

4 These delicious tree fruits are a good prize for my effort! Trees bear fruit all year round in the rain forest, so I always have something good to eat.

Near the tip, my tail has no fur underneath. Instead, it has strong skin like my hands— perfect for gripping things.

Here I made my tail into a bridge!

My tail can hold all my weight. So I can hang from a branch for a drink above the water. My hands are free for other things, like picking fruit.

How do Animals Survive in the Desert?

I am an addax, a type of antelope. I live in the Sahara Desert. I live most of my life without drinking. I get all the water I need from dew and the plants that I eat, like grass and leaves.

I am a jerboa. I am like mice and rats, but I can jump like a kangaroo. I rest under the ground during the day and come out at night to eat.

I am a fennec fox. I hide from the day's heat in my cool hole. My big ears give off heat and help me cool down.

We camels have two-toed feet with soft pads that spread out when we take steps. That's how we can walk on the loose sand. I can walk about 25 miles (40 km) a day.

I am a male sandgrouse. Every day, I fly many miles (km) to find water. I soak my feathers with water so my chicks can drink from them.

Living in the desert is tough for all of us, but we have some clever ways of surviving in such a hot, dry place. I am a dromedary camel. I can go without water for months. When I do find water, I can drink about 30 gallons (114 l) at one time!

I close my nostrils to keep sand out.

My long eyelashes also stop sand from getting in my eyes.

My hump doesn't hold water. It stores fat that my body makes into food when I need it.

I move so that only one small patch of skin touches the hot sand at a time. You can see why I'm called a sidewinder.

When it's too hot for us horned vipers, we bury ourselves in sand. See my horns there?

What Do Bats Eat?

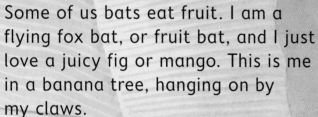

Some of us bats eat fruit. I am a flying fox bat, or fruit bat, and I just love a juicy fig or mango. This is me in a banana tree, hanging on by my claws.

I am a vampire bat, and I drink blood! I bite an animal's skin with my sharp teeth and drink up.

I am a pollinating bat. Like a bee, I spread pollen from flower to flower while I eat. While I lick the sweet nectar, the pollen gets on my fur. When I move on, the pollen comes, too.

From the echoes, we can detect nearby prey. We can also guess how far away prey is, how fast it is moving, and in which direction.

18

Most bats hunt mainly at night, gliding silently on their leathery wings. We don't need our eyes to know where we are. Instead, we use sound to help us fly and hunt in the dark. We make high-pitched squeaks and listen for the echoes.

Long-eared bats, like me, also use echoes to see.

I am a leaf-nosed bat. The ridges around my nose and mouth help bring the sounds of echoes to my ears.

I am a fisherman bat. I catch fish swimming just below the surface of lakes and rivers with my claws. I can hear the fish swimming from the ripples on the water. Then I strike!

Most bats are nocturnal. That means they come out at night to hunt, and sleep during the day. They live in large groups, usually in dark places like caves, trees, or the roofs of buildings. They hang upside down to sleep and even to nurse their young.

How Does a Bird Fly?

We are not just ducks. We are some of the world's most wonderful flying machines! Our secret is the shape of our chest and wings. We have very large chest muscles. These give us the power to beat our wings strongly. Did you know that ducks are among the fastest-flying birds on Earth? Only swifts are faster than us.

We tuck our legs and feet under us when we fly so they don't slow us down.

Air passing over my curved wings lifts me up. My feathers make my shape smooth so I move easily through the air.

My tail helps me balance and steer.

All of us birds have light bones that are full of airholes like a honeycomb. We also have lightweight beaks.

We ducks fly in a V-shape formation, with one duck at the front and the others behind. The lead duck cuts a path through the air, making it easier for those behind to fly. We take turns leading because it's very tiring.

Flapping our wings pushes us forward and keeps us in the air at the same time. Ducks have short, pointed wings that are good for building up speed, but not for gliding. We have to flap them all the time or we would drop out of the sky!

Birds like albatrosses and eagles have much larger wings. They allow them to glide on air currents without flapping for hours on end.

Flapping is very hard work. It uses up more energy than running or swimming. We need lots of oxygen to keep our muscles going, so we have very strong lungs. Ours take more oxygen out of the air than yours do.

These stiff feathers on my wings are called flight feathers. I can spread them out or angle them to move forward, steer, or to slow myself down.

I'm a ruby-throated hummingbird. Instead of flying, I hover. I hold perfectly still while I lick nectar from flowers with my long tongue. I beat my stiff wings around 50 times every second. I can even fly backward!

How Do Birds Attract a Mate?

I'm a sage grouse. When it's time for me to find a mate, I strut around, fan out my tail feathers, and puff up my chest. By blowing air into two yellow sacks under my throat, I can make a loud cracking noise to impress the females.

The most important thing that we animals have to do is find a mate and to give birth to our babies. It's mostly up to male birds to win over a female. Some birds have excellent ways of doing this, and we peacocks are the most excellent of them all.

During the mating season, we red-plumed birds of paradise gather to display our beautiful feathers. Females have very dull brown feathers to camouflage them while they are sitting on their nests.

We bald eagles tumble and dive through the air with our partners in a midair mating dance. We sometimes lock talons as we spin high above the ground.

Bald eagles mate for life. We'll repeat this dance with our partners each year in the mating season. Once we have mated, we both care for the eggs by keeping them warm and feeding our babies when they hatch.

Red-crowned cranes also mate for life, so our mating dance is a very important way of finding the right partner.

23

How Does an Owl Hunt at Night?

I am a tawny owl, a silent, sneaky hunter. You'll find tawnies, like me, gliding after our prey at night, throughout Europe and parts of Asia. The feathers on my broad wings have soft edges. They dampen the flapping noise that wings usually make so that my prey doesn't hear me.

My big eyes are good for seeing in the dark. I turn my head right around to look behind me.

1 My hearing is so good I can find and catch prey just by listening, without ever seeing it.

2 When I see or hear prey, I swoop in to get closer. I use my wings to change direction as I follow my prey.

My talons are long, sharp, and powerful. I have four toes. When I'm flying, three of them face forwards, and one backwards. When I clutch prey, one toe swivels around to the back to improve my grip.

We normally lay up to five eggs, which hatch in the order they were laid. Baby owls are covered in soft feathers. We keep feeding them for several weeks until their adult feathers grow.

Owls have no teeth and cannot chew food, so we swallow our prey whole. We eat things like fur, feathers, teeth and bone, which we cannot digest. So we cough up these remains in a small, neat ball called a pellet.

We can't eat again until we cough it up.

4 I'm almost there! I have almost stopped in midair. I swing my legs forward and open my talons.

3 Fanning out my wing and tail feathers slows me down.

5 This little vole won't know what has hit it until it's too late.

6 Now I'll fly away to a quiet place to enjoy my dinner. I can swallow prey this size in a single gulp. I hold bigger prey firmly in my talons and tear it into bite-sized chunks with my sharp, curved beak. I eat many things: small mammals, frogs, birds, insects, worms, and even fish.

How Does a Tadpole Become a Frog?

We frogs are amphibians. That means we spend part of our lives on land and part in the water. We need to lay our eggs in water. We also need to keep our skin moist to help us breathe. That's because our lungs are very small, so we must take in air through our skin. On land, we like to live in cool, damp places.

2 When we tadpoles first hatch, we feed on what's left of our eggs, along with tiny water plants called algae. Like fish, we breathe through openings in our heads called gills. Gradually, these disappear as our lungs grow. Now we can breathe air.

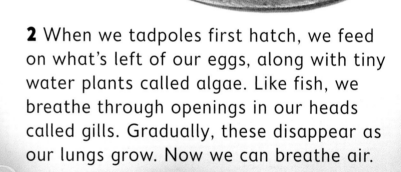

1 Frogs' eggs are called spawn. Females lay thousands of eggs at a time. Thick jelly keeps the eggs moist and provides food for the growing tadpoles. Animals, such as fish and diving beetles, will eat frogspawn, but there are so many eggs that at least some will live on. The black dots will soon start to turn into tadpoles.

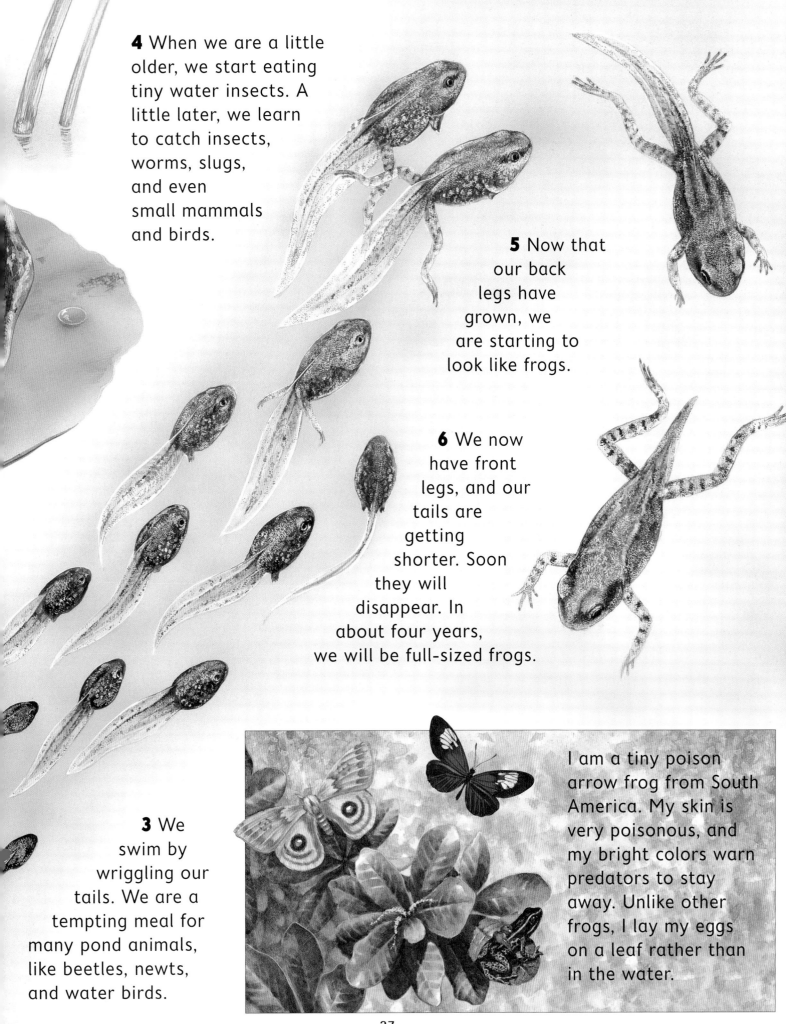

4 When we are a little older, we start eating tiny water insects. A little later, we learn to catch insects, worms, slugs, and even small mammals and birds.

5 Now that our back legs have grown, we are starting to look like frogs.

6 We now have front legs, and our tails are getting shorter. Soon they will disappear. In about four years, we will be full-sized frogs.

3 We swim by wriggling our tails. We are a tempting meal for many pond animals, like beetles, newts, and water birds.

I am a tiny poison arrow frog from South America. My skin is very poisonous, and my bright colors warn predators to stay away. Unlike other frogs, I lay my eggs on a leaf rather than in the water.

27

How Does a Snake Capture Its Prey?

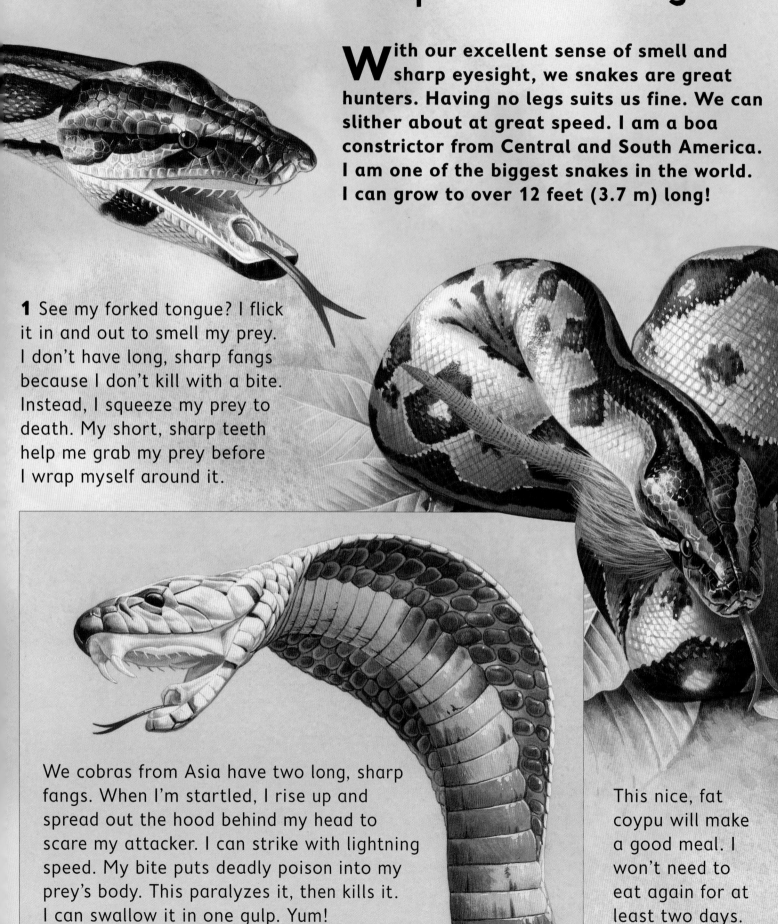

With our excellent sense of smell and sharp eyesight, we snakes are great hunters. Having no legs suits us fine. We can slither about at great speed. I am a boa constrictor from Central and South America. I am one of the biggest snakes in the world. I can grow to over 12 feet (3.7 m) long!

1 See my forked tongue? I flick it in and out to smell my prey. I don't have long, sharp fangs because I don't kill with a bite. Instead, I squeeze my prey to death. My short, sharp teeth help me grab my prey before I wrap myself around it.

We cobras from Asia have two long, sharp fangs. When I'm startled, I rise up and spread out the hood behind my head to scare my attacker. I can strike with lightning speed. My bite puts deadly poison into my prey's body. This paralyzes it, then kills it. I can swallow it in one gulp. Yum!

This nice, fat coypu will make a good meal. I won't need to eat again for at least two days.

I'm a copperhead pit viper from America. I attract animals, like this frog, with my tail's yellow tip. Then I strike with my fangs.

Green vine snakes, like me, can hide very well. I look exactly like the branches of the trees I live in. I drop down onto my prey, like this lizard, grab it by the neck, and squeeze. My bite is poisonous, but my prey often suffocate first.

3 I can unhinge my jaw to fit large prey into my mouth. I swallow it whole, head first.

2 Once I have grabbed my prey, I just wind myself around it and squeeze. When it's dead, I'll unwrap myself and chow down.

How Does a Crocodile Raise Its Young?

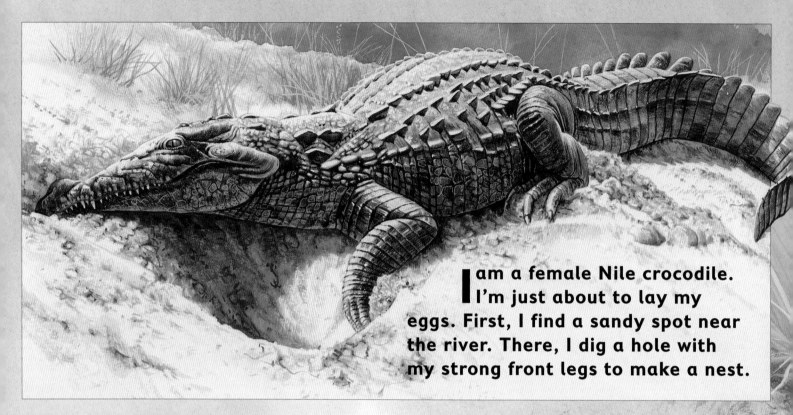

I am a female Nile crocodile. I'm just about to lay my eggs. First, I find a sandy spot near the river. There, I dig a hole with my strong front legs to make a nest.

2 I guard my nest for three months until the eggs hatch. Monitor lizards, meerkats, or rats might try to steal the eggs if I leave them alone.

1 I lay between 15 and 80 eggs. Smooth and white with hard shells, they are each about the size of a chicken's egg. I cover them with sand to keep them warm and dry.

3 When my babies start squeaking from inside their eggs, it's time for me to dig them out.

4 My mate and I help the babies hatch by rolling the eggs around inside our mouths.

5 When there is danger, I pick up my babies with my teeth, toss them in the air, and catch them again in my mouth.

6 My babies are safe in my mouth, as long as I remember not to swallow! They can swim as soon as they hatch.

7 I'll keep my babies close to me for up to two months. Insects, frogs, and small fish are their food. The babies grow about 1 foot (30 cm) each year. But, in spite of all my care, only one or two will live to become adults.

Glossary

camouflage
(KA-muh-flahj) The colors and marks that help an animal hide.

gills (GILZ) The body parts used by some animals to breathe underwater.

hibernation
(hy-bur-NAY-shun) The deep sleep that some animals go into over the cold winter months.

paralyzes
(PER-uh-lyz-ez) Stopping prey from moving by poisoning it.

pollinating
(PAH-luh-nayt-ing) Moving pollen around to different plants, which helps them make seeds.

predators
(PREH-duh-terz) Animals that hunt and kill other animals for food.

savanna (suh-VA-nuh) An area of grasslands with few bushes and trees.

scavengers
(SKA-ven-jurz) Animals that feed on the remains of food killed by other animals.

Index

Web Sites

Due to the changing nature of Internet links, PowerKids Press has developed an online list of Web sites related to the subject of this book. This site is updated regularly. Please use this link to access the list: www.powerkidslinks.com/ask/animal/